PowerKids Readers:

The Bilingual Library of the
United States of America™

NORTH DAKOTA
DAKOTA DEL NORTE

VANESSA BROWN

TRADUCCIÓN AL ESPAÑOL: MARÍA CRISTINA BRUSCA

The Rosen Publishing Group's
PowerKids Press™ & **Editorial Buenas Letras**™
New York

Published in 2006 by The Rosen Publishing Group, Inc.
29 East 21st Street, New York, NY 10010

First Edition

Book Design: Albert B. Hanner
Photo Credits: Cover © Tom Bean/Corbis; pp. 5, 31 (Thompson) © Albert B. Hanner; p. 7 © 2002 Geoatlas; pp. 9, 30 (nickname), 31 (prairie) © Richard Hamilton Smith/Corbis; p. 11 © Geoffrey Clements/Corbis; pp. 13, 15, 31 (pelt) (Morris) © Bettmann/Corbis; p. 17 © Najiah Feanny/Corbis SABA; pp. 19, 21, 30 (motto) © Tom Bean/Corbis; pp. 23, 31 (dam) © Annie Griffiths Belt/Corbis; p.p. 25, 30 (capital) © Joseph Sohm; Chromosohm Inc./Corbis; p. 30 (flower) © Annie Griffiths Belt/Corbis, (bird) © Darrell Gulin/Corbis, (tree) © W. Perry Conway/Corbis; pp. 31 (Sitting Bull) © Corbis, (Lamour) © Roger Ressmeyer/Corbis, (Christopher) © David Turnley/Corbis, (Dickenson) © Hulton-Deutsch Collection/Corbis.

Library of Congress Cataloging-in-Publication Data

Brown, Vanessa, 1963–
North Dakota = Dakota del Norte / Vanessa Brown ; traducción al español, María Cristina Brusca.— 1st ed.
p. cm. — (The bilingual library of the United States of America) Includes bibliographical references and index.
ISBN 1-4042-3099-8 (library binding)
1. North Dakota–Juvenile literature. I. Title: Dakota del Norte. II. Title. III. Series.
F636.3.B76 2006
978.4-dc22
                                        2005020505

Manufactured in the United States of America

Due to the changing nature of Internet links, Editorial Buenas Letras has developed an online list of Web sites related to the subject of this book. This site is updated regularly. Please use this link to access the list:

http://www.buenasletraslinks.com/ls/northdakota

Contents

Contenido

Welcome to North Dakota

These are the flag and seal of the state of North Dakota. In the center of the flag there is a bald eagle. The bald eagle is the national bird of the United States.

Bienvenidos a Dakota del Norte

Estos son la bandera y el escudo de Dakota del Norte. En el centro de la bandera hay un águila calva. El águila calva es el ave nacional de los Estados Unidos.

North Dakota Flag and State Seal

Bandera y escudo de Dakota del Norte

North Dakota Geography

North Dakota borders the states of Montana, Minnesota, and South Dakota. North Dakota shares a border with the country of Canada.

Geografía de Dakota del Norte

Dakota del Norte linda con los estados de Montana, Minnesota y Dakota del Sur. Dakota del Norte comparte una frontera con otro país, Canadá.

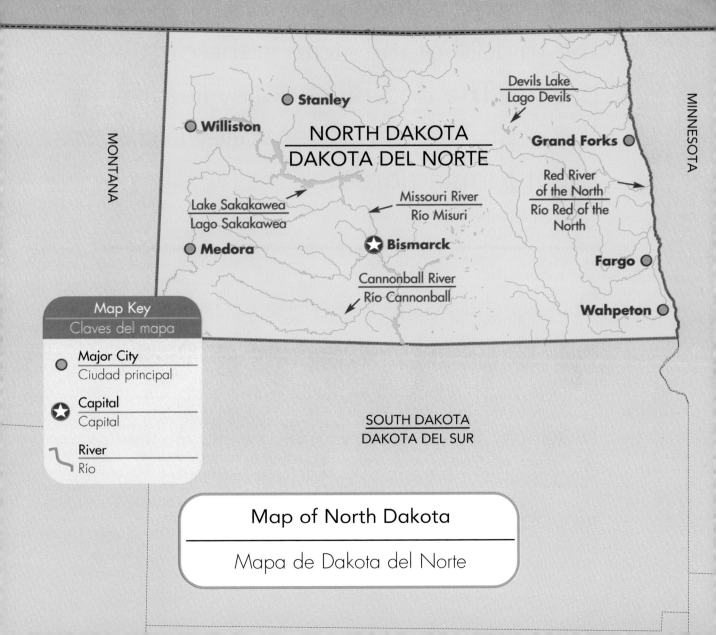

CANADA
CANADÁ

MONTANA

Stanley

Williston

Devils Lake
Lago Devils

NORTH DAKOTA
DAKOTA DEL NORTE

Grand Forks

MINNESOTA

Lake Sakakawea
Lago Sakakawea

Missouri River
Río Misuri

Red River
of the North
Río Red of the
North

Medora

Bismarck

Fargo

Cannonball River
Río Cannonball

Wahpeton

Map Key
Claves del mapa

Major City
Ciudad principal

Capital
Capital

River
Río

SOUTH DAKOTA
DAKOTA DEL SUR

Map of North Dakota

Mapa de Dakota del Norte

North Dakota has three land areas. In the west is the Great Plains. In the middle of the state is the drift prairie. The Red River valley lies in the east. The Red River valley is a great farming area.

Dakota del Norte tiene tres grandes regiones. En el oeste está la Gran Llanura. En la zona central está la pradera. En el este se encuentra el Valle Red River. El Valle Red River es una región excelente para la agricultura.

Green Wheat Field in Red River Valley

Campo de cultivo de trigo en el Valle Red River

North Dakota History

Fur trade was the most important activity in North Dakota in the 1800s. Mandan and Hidatsa Indians lived near the Knife River. They traded animal pelts for food with French explorers.

Historia de Dakota del Norte

El intercambio de pieles fue la actividad más importante de Dakota del Norte, en los años 1800. Los grupos indígenas Hidatsa y Mandan vivían cerca del río Knife. Estas tribus les cambiaban pieles de animales por comida a los exploradores franceses.

Mandan Indians on a Frozen River

Indios Mandan en un río congelado

In 1805, Meriwether Lewis and William Clark passed through what is now North Dakota. Lewis and Clark were looking for the western territories. They traveled from Missouri to the Pacific Ocean.

En 1805, Meriwether Lewis y William Clark entraron en la región que hoy es Dakota del Norte. Lewis y Clark buscaban una ruta hacia los territorios occidentales. Lewis y Clark viajaron desde Misuri hasta el océano Pacífico.

Lewis and Clark Trip

El viaje de Lewis y Clark

Sacagawea was a Shoshone Indian. She joined Lewis and Clark in their trip to the West. Sacagawea knew the land and many Native American languages. She was a great help to Lewis and Clark.

Sacagawea fue una india Shoshone que se unió a Lewis y Clark en su viaje hacia el oeste. Sacagawea conocía el terreno y muchas lenguas indígenas. Sus conocimientos fueron una gran ayuda para Lewis y Clark.

Sacagawea Guiding Lewis and Clark

Sacagawea guía a Lewis y Clark

In the winter of 1997, snow and heavy rain flooded the Missouri River and the Red River of the North. This was the biggest flood in North Dakota's history.

En el invierno de 1997, la nieve y las fuertes lluvias desbordaron los ríos Misuri y Red. Esto provocó las inundaciones más grandes de la historia de Dakota del Norte.

Grand Forks, North Dakota

Grand Forks, Dakota del Norte

Living in North Dakota

Native Americans in North Dakota honor their history with powwows. A powwow is a big party with dance and music.

La vida en Dakota del Norte

Los nativos americanos de Dakota del Norte preservan su historia realizando *powwows*. Un *powwow* es una gran fiesta con música y danza.

Powwow Dancers at Fort Totten, Bismarck

Danzantes en un powwow, en Fort Totten, Bismarck

Farming is important for North Dakota. The state produces more sunflowers, oats, canola, and dry beans than any other state. The chief crop produced in North Dakota is wheat.

La agricultura es importante para Dakota del Norte. El estado produce más girasol, avena, canola y frijoles secos que cualquier otro estado. El trigo es el mayor cultivo de Dakota del Norte.

Gathering Wheat

Cosecha de trigo

In 1947, North Dakota began building the Garrison Dam on the Missouri River. The dam was finished in 1960. The building of the Garrison Dam produced Lake Sakakawea.

En 1947, Dakota del Norte comenzó la construcción de la presa Garrison, en el río Misuri. La presa se terminó en 1960. La construcción de la presa Garrison creó el lago Sakakawea.

View of Garrison Dam

Vista de la presa Garrison

Fargo, Grand Forks, Bismarck, and Minot are important cities in North Dakota. Bismarck is the capital of the state.

Fargo, Grand Forks, Bismarck y Minot son ciudades importantes de Dakota del Norte. Bismarck es la capital del estado.

State Capitol Building in Bismarck

Capitolio del estado, en Bismarck

Activity:
Let's Draw North Dakota's State Fish

The northern pike is North Dakota's state fish.

Actividad:
Dibujemos el pez de Dakota del Norte

El lucio del norte es el pez del estado de Dakota del Norte.

1

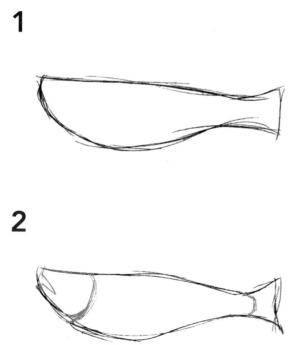

Draw a straight line on the top and a curved line on the bottom. The right side will be the tail.

Dibuja una línea recta en la parte superior y una línea curva en la parte inferior. El lado derecho será la cola.

2

For the head draw a curved vertical line. Draw the mouth. Next draw a curved line for the tail.

Para dibujar la cabeza traza una línea curva vertical. Dibuja la boca. Luego traza una línea curva para representar la cola.

3

For the eye draw a circle and then draw a smaller circle inside. Draw five fins on the side of the fish.

En el lugar del ojo traza un círculo y luego, dibuja adentro otro círculo más pequeño. Dibuja cinco aletas en el costado del pez.

4

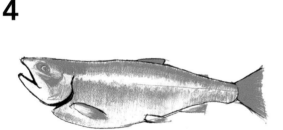

Erase extra lines. Now begin shading. Hold your pencil on its side and lightly shade the fish. Notice that some parts of the fish are darker than others.

Borra las líneas extras. Ahora comienza a sombrear. Tomando el lápiz de costado, sombrea suavemente el pez. Fíjate que algunas partes del pez son más oscuras que otras.

Timeline		Cronología
The Cheyenne occupied the Sheyenne River valley.	**A. D. 1600**	La tribu Cheyenne ocupa el valle del río Sheyenne.
The Louisiana Purchase transfers the area of North Dakota from France to the United States.	**1803**	La Compra de Luisiana transfiere a los Estados Unidos la región de Dakota del Norte que pertenecía a Francia.
Meriwether Lewis and William Clark enter North Dakota on their way to the Pacific coast.	**1804**	Meriwether Lewis y William Clark, en camino hacia la costa del Pacífico, entran en la región de Dakota del Norte.
North Dakota becomes the thirty-ninth state.	**1889**	Dakota del Norte es admitida en la Unión como el estado treinta y nueve.
The place for the International Peace Garden is picked in North Dakota and Manitoba.	**1931**	Se selecciona el sitio para la construcción del Jardín Internacional de la Paz en Dakota del Norte y Manitoba.
The Garrison Dam is completed and Lake Sakakawea is finished.	**1960**	Se completa la presa Garrison y se forma el lago Sakakawea.

North Dakota Events/
Eventos en Dakota del Norte

March
North Dakota Winter Show
in Valley City

June
Fort Seward Wagon Train in
Jamestown
Medora Musical in Medora

July
Governor's Cup Walleye Fishing
Tournament on Lake Sakagawea
North Dakota State Fair in Minot

August
Champion's Ride Rodeo in Sentinel
Butte

September
Potato Bowl in Grand Forks
United Tribes International Powwow
in Bismarck
Sodbuster Days at Fort Ransom
State Park

December
Country Christmas at Bonanzaville,
USA, in West Fargo

Marzo
Exposición invernal de Dakota del Norte,
en Valley City

Junio
Caravana de Fort Seward, en Jamestown
Medora Musical, en Medora

Julio
Copa Gobernador del torneo de pesca
de Walleye, en el lago Sacagawea
Feria del estado de Dakota del Norte, en
Minot

Agosto
Rodeo de Campeones, en Sentinel Butte

Septiembre
Potato Bowl, en Grand Forks
Powwow Internacional de las Tribus
Unidas, en Bismarck
Sodbuster Days, en el Parque Estatal Fort
Ransom

Diciembre
Navidad campestre, en Bonanzaville
E.U.A., en West Fargo

North Dakota Facts/
Datos sobre Dakota Del Norte

<u>Population</u>
642,000

<u>Población</u>
642,000

<u>Capital</u>
Bismarck

<u>Capital</u>
Bismarck

<u>State Motto</u>
Under God the People
Rule

<u>Lema del estado</u>
El pueblo gobierna debajo
de Dios

<u>State Flower</u>
Wild Prairie Rose

<u>Flor del estado</u>
Rosa silvestre de la pradera

<u>State Bird</u>
Western Meadowlark

<u>Ave del estado</u>
Pradero occidental

<u>State Nickname</u>
Flickertail State

<u>Mote del estado</u>
Estado Flickertail

<u>State Tree</u>
American Elm

<u>Árbol del estado</u>
Olmo americano

<u>State Song</u>
"North Dakota Hymn"

<u>Canción del estado</u>
"Himno a Dakota del Norte"

Famous North Dakota/
Nordakoteños famosos

Sitting Bull
(1831–1890)

Sioux leader
Líder Sioux

Era Bell Thompson
(1905–1985)

Editor
Editora

Louis L'Amour
(1908–1988)

Author
Escritor

Warren Christopher
(1925–)

U.S. secretary of state
Secretario de estado de E.U.A.

Angie Dickinson
(1932–)

Actress
Actriz

Roger Eugene Maris
(1934–1985)

Baseball player
Jugador de béisbol

Words to Know/Palabras que debes saber

border
frontera

dam
presa

pelt
piel

prairie
pradera

31

Here are more books to read about North Dakota:
Otros libros que puedes leer sobre Dakota del Norte:

In English/En inglés:

North Dakota
America the Beautiful
by Hintz Martin
Children's Press, 2000

North Dakota
Hello USA
by Verba Joan Marie
Lerner Publishing group, 2002

Words in English: 331

Palabras en español: 365

Index

Índice